Animal Detectives

Search for the Facts

BIG CATS

Anne O'Daly

raintree
a Capstone company — publishers for children

Raintree is an imprint of Capstone Global Library Limited, a company incorporated in England and Wales having its registered office at 264 Banbury Road, Oxford, OX2 7DY - Registered company number: 6695582

www.raintree.co.uk
myorders@raintree.co.uk

Ths edition published by Raintree in 2021

Created by Brown Bear Books Ltd
Design Manager: Keith Davis
Children's Publisher: Anne O'Daly
Picture Manager: Sophie Mortimer
Printed and bound in India

ISBN 978 1 4747 9845 7 (hardback)
ISBN 978 1 4747 9851 8 (paperback)

British Library Cataloguing in Publication Data
A full catalogue record for this book is available from the British Library.

Picture Credits
Cover: Shutterstock: Vladimir Wrangel; Interior: iStock: abzerit 16, Ken Canning 4-5b, Freder 4-5c, GOLFX 5tr(inset), istiv 4l, Kinwun 4bl, Maggy Meyer 5tl, mlenny 5r, THEPALMER 8; Shutterstock: COULANGES 20, David Hoffmann Photography 5tr, Dennis W Donohue 19, Andreya Gudkov 12, Lorri Kajena, 18-19, 22, Christina Li 1, 3, 8-9, 12-13, 14-15, 22, 23, Lookingforcats 6, Matt Porter Wildlife 14, Atthapol Sailta 10, TLWilson Photography 5br.
t=top, r=right, l=left, c=centre, b=bottom
All artwork and other photography Brown Bear Books.

Contents

Meet the family

Big cats are powerful hunters. They have strong bodies and sharp teeth. Big cats are related to pet cats. They are both mammals. Read on to find out more!

Lion

Bobcat

Leopards are good climbers. They spend most of their lives in trees.

Leopard

Snow leopard

Lion

Lions are built to hunt. They have sharp teeth and claws. Males are bigger than females, but females are better at hunting.

FACT FILE

Scientific name:
Panthera leo

Food: antelope, giraffe, zebra, buffalo

Habitat: grassland, woodland

Where in the world: Africa and India

a female lion is called a lioness

long thin tail with a tuft at the end

Lions live in a group called a pride.

WHERE DOES IT LIVE?

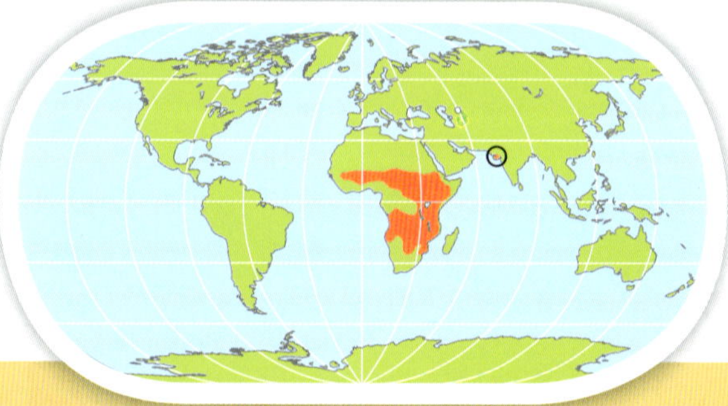

BIG OR SMALL

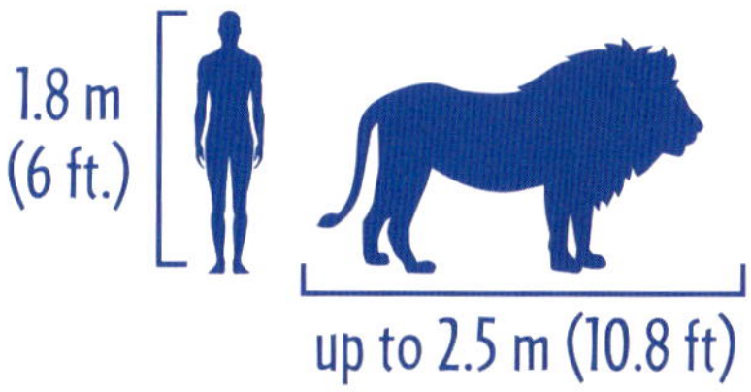

Lions are loud! You can hear them roar from 8 kilometres (5 miles) away.

Tiger

Tigers are the biggest cats in the world. They hunt at night. They creep up on prey. Then they pounce on it and kill it.

FACT FILE

Scientific name: *Panthera tigris*

Food: deer, buffalo, antelope

Habitat: forests and swamps

Where in the world: India, Southeast Asia, China, south-east Russia

Stripes help tigers hide in long grass. Each tiger has its own pattern of stripes.

WHERE DOES IT LIVE?

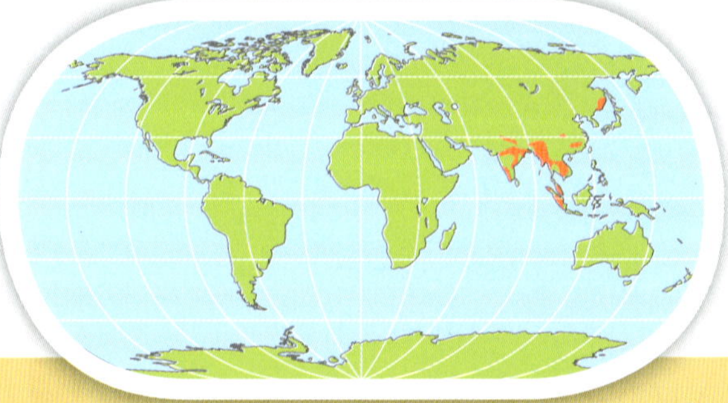

BIG OR SMALL

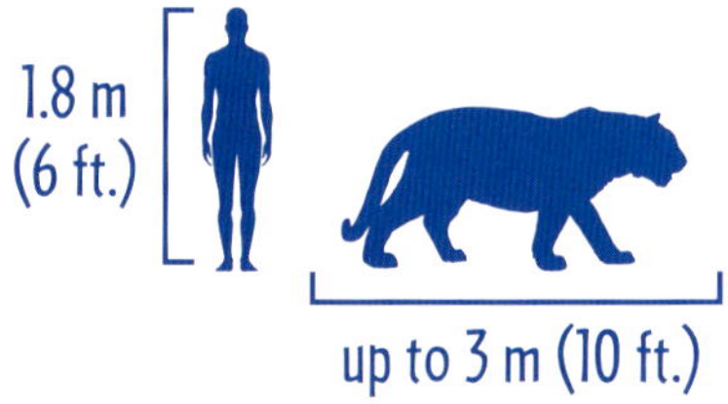

Some tigers have white fur and black stripes. They are very rare. Only 1 in 10,000 tigers is white.

Jaguar

Jaguars live in Central and South America. They have powerful jaws and sharp teeth. They can crunch through hard turtle shells.

FACT FILE

Scientific name: *Panthera onca*

Food: wild pigs, capybaras, turtles, fish, crocodiles

Habitat: forest, swamps, grasslands, deserts

Where in the world: Central and South America

Jaguars like to live near water. They are good swimmers.

WHERE DOES IT LIVE?

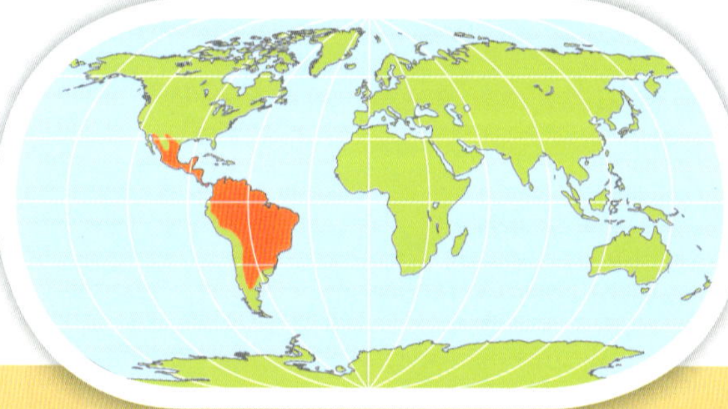

Jaguars live alone. They only come together to mate. Cubs stay with their mother for two years.

BIG OR SMALL

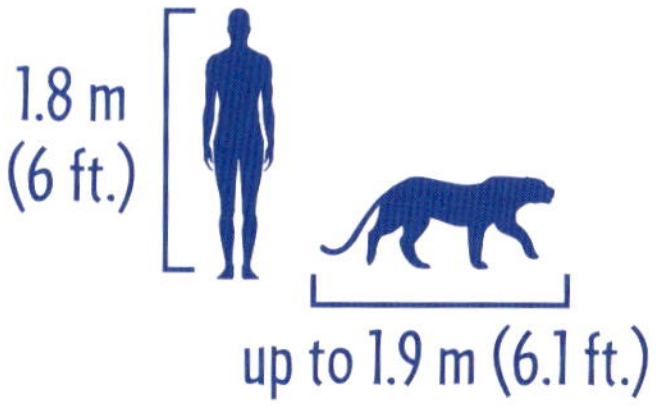

Cheetah

Cheetahs are built for speed. They are the fastest animals on land. Their top speed is 113 km/h (70 mph).

FACT FILE

Scientific name:
Acinonyx jubatus

Food: small and medium-sized mammals (gazelles and impalas)

Habitat: grassland, scrubland and semi-desert

Where in the world: Africa and the Middle East

Cubs stay with their mother for about six months.

WHERE DOES IT LIVE?

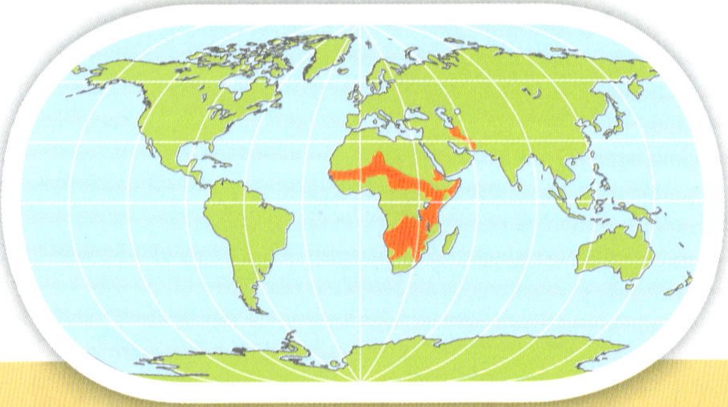

Cheetahs run at top speed for one minute. Then they have to stop and rest.

BIG OR SMALL

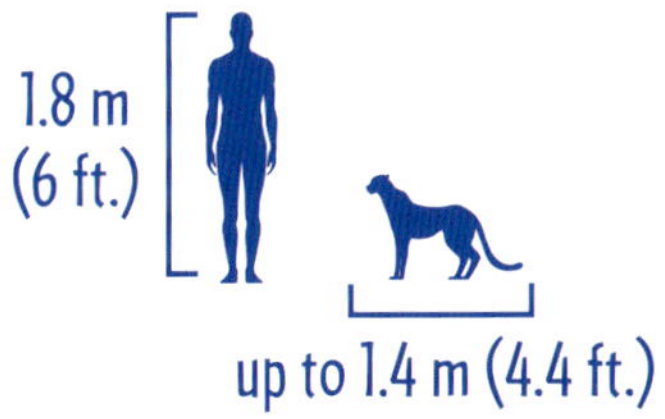

Leopard

The leopard is the best climber of all the big cats. It rests in a tree during the day. It comes down at night to hunt.

FACT FILE

Scientific name:
Panthera pardus

Food: gazelles, impalas, monkeys, rabbits, wild pigs, insects

Habitat: forests, grasslands, semi-desert

Where in the world: Africa, South Asia, Arabia, Far East

Leopards' spots are called rosettes. They look like roses.

WHERE DOES IT LIVE?

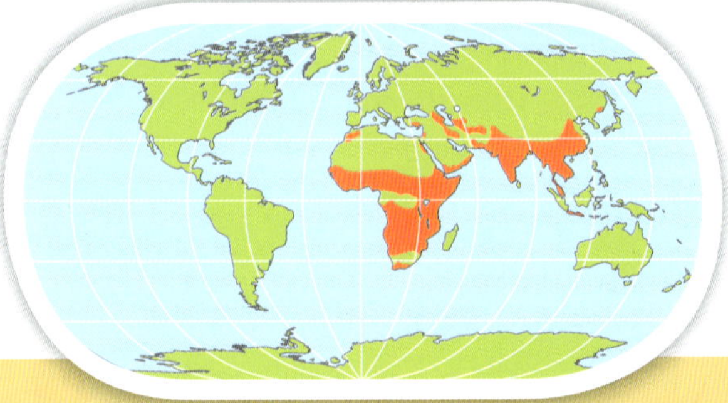

Leopards are good jumpers. They can spring forward 6 metres (20 feet). They can jump up 3 metres (10 feet) in the air.

BIG OR SMALL

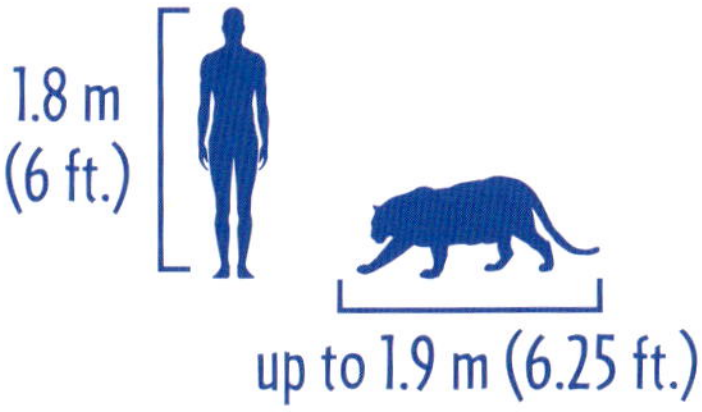

Snow leopard

This cat lives in cold mountains. A thick coat of fur keeps it warm. The bottom of its feet are furry!

FACT FILE

Scientific name:
Uncia uncial

Food: mountain goats, deer, marmots, pikas

Habitat: rocky mountains

Where in the world: China, India, Pakistan, Nepal, Russia

long tail for balance

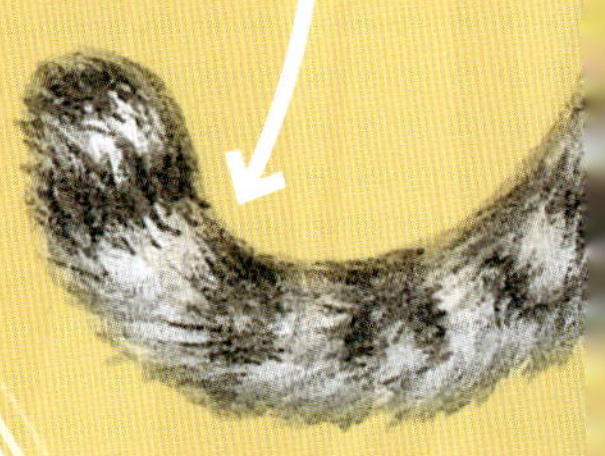

The colours and patterns are good camouflage in the snow.

WHERE DOES IT LIVE?

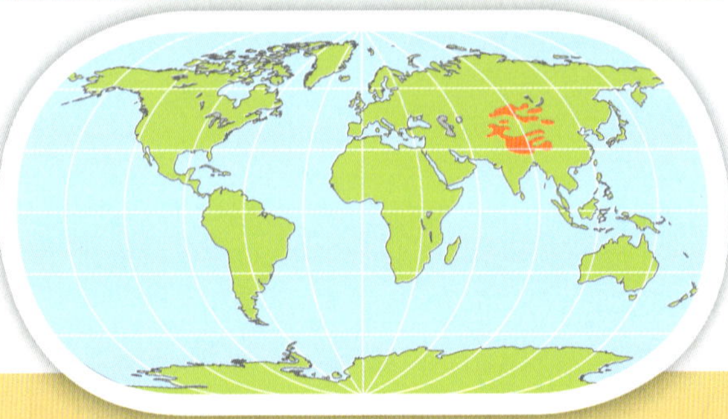

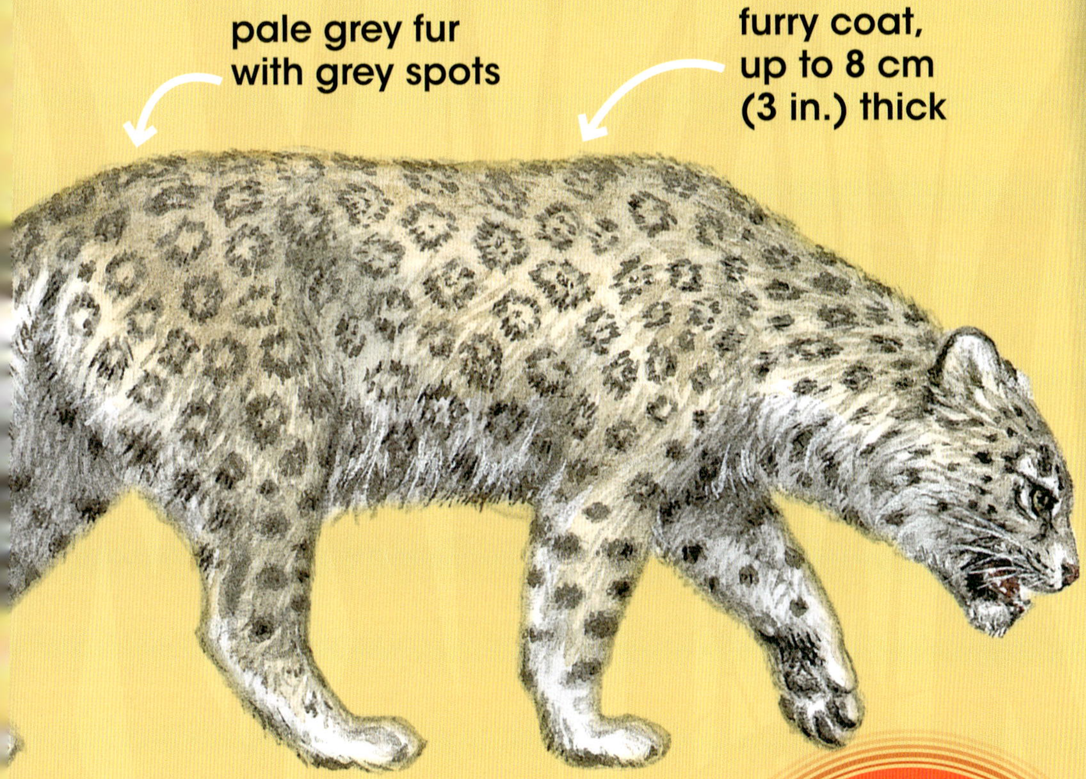

BIG OR SMALL

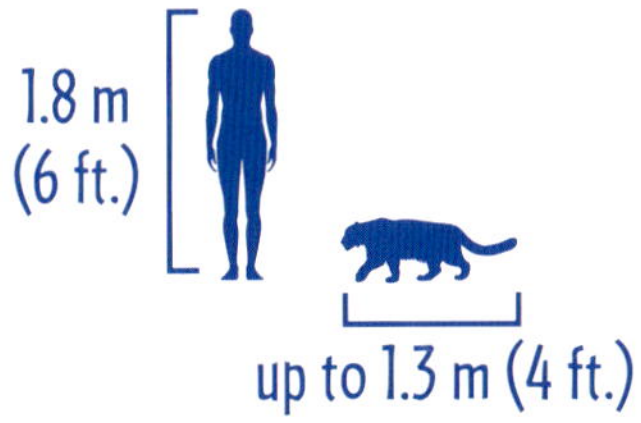

The snow leopard has a long, thick tail. It wraps its tail around its body. This keeps it warm.

Mountain lion

Mountain lions hide in trees. They wait for prey to go past. Then they jump down and attack.

FACT FILE

Scientific name:
Puma concolor

Food: deer, rodents, hares

Habitat: forests, swamps, grasslands, mountains

Where in the world: North and South America

Mountain lions have lots of names. They are also called pumas, cougars, panthers and catamounts.

WHERE DOES IT LIVE?

A mountain lion pounces on prey in the snow.

BIG OR SMALL

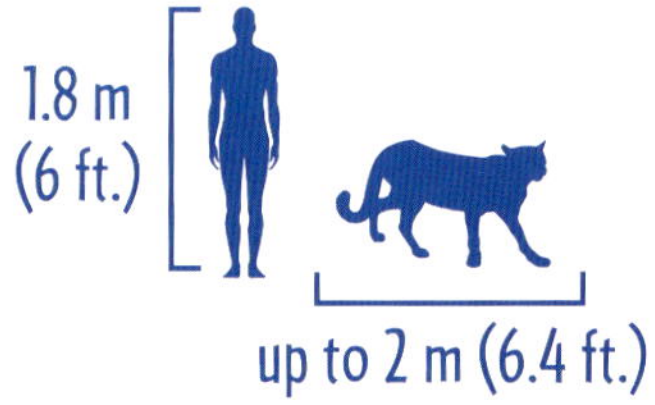

Bobcat

Bobcats look like big pussy cats. But they are fierce. They creep up on prey. They attack with a sudden leap.

FACT FILE

Scientific name:
Lynx rufus

Food: mainly rabbits and hares, but also deer, birds, wild pigs, beavers

Habitat: forests, swamp, mountains, at the edge of deserts

Where in the world: North America

Bobcats have a short, bobbed tail. That gives them their name.

WHERE DOES IT LIVE?

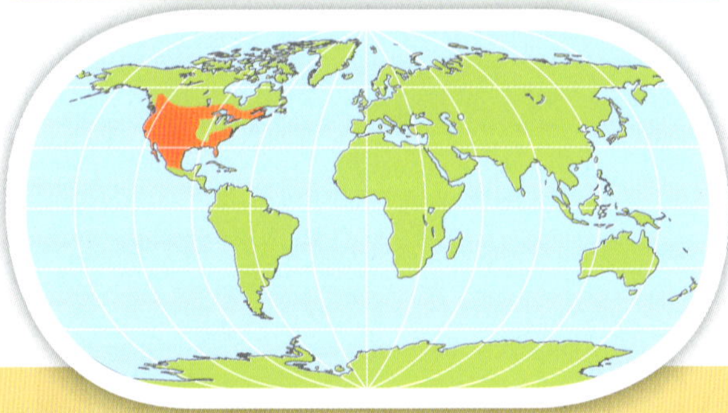

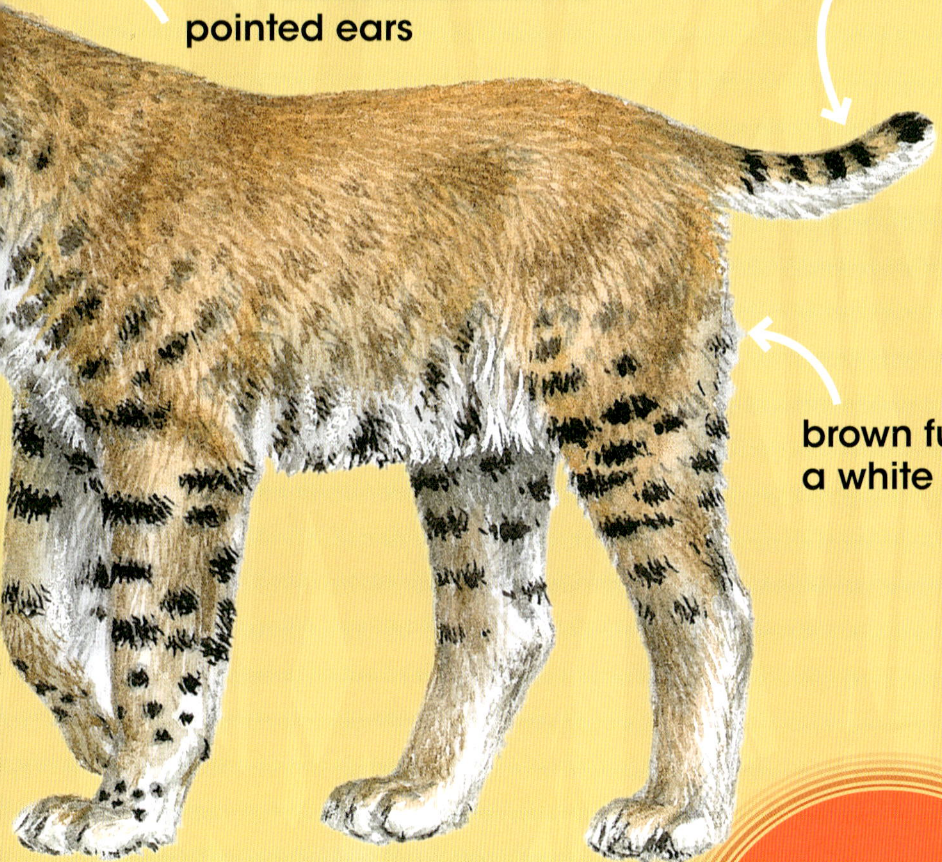

pointed ears

short tail with black bands

brown fur and a white belly

BIG OR SMALL

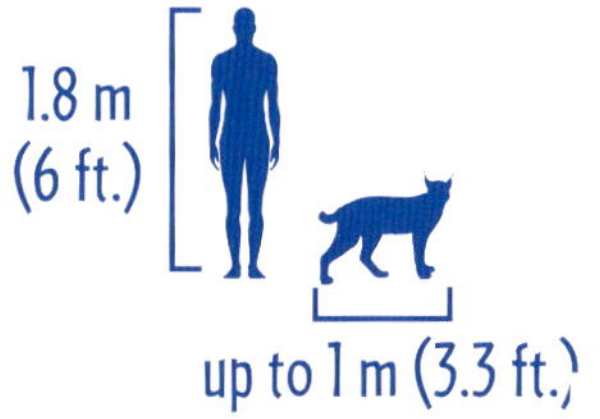

Bobcats hunt at night. They rest in a den in the day. They have one main den and some smaller ones.

Quiz

Test your skills! Can you answer these questions? Look in the book for clues. The answers are on page 24.

2 How does the bobcat get its name?

1 How thick is a snow leopard's fur?

4 What are some other names for mountain lions?

3 What do a tiger's stripes do?

Glossary

camouflage
Colours and patterns that blend into the background.

cub
The name for a big cat's baby.

den
Where an animal rests or sleeps.

habitat
The kind of place where an animal usually lives.

mammal
An animal that feeds its young on milk. Most mammals have fur or hair.

prey
An animal that is hunted by another animal for food.

Find out more

Books

Big Cats (DKfindout!), (DK Children, 2019)

It's All About ... Wild Cats, (Kingfisher, 2017)

Websites

animalfactsencyclopedia.com/Big-cat-facts.html

easyscienceforkids.com/all-about-the-cat-family/

online.kidsdiscover.com/unit/big-cats

Index

Quiz answers: 1. Its fur is up to 8 centimetres (3 inches) long. **2.** It is named after its short, bobbed tail. **3.** The stripes help the tiger hide in long grass. **4.** Pumas, cougars, panthers and catamounts.